Five-Minute
SUNDay SCHOOL
ACTiViTies

EXPLORING THE BIBLE

Mary J. Davis

To Larry and our children.
To John and Mary; Ron and Robin; David and Linda; Phil and Kim; Barb and Larry; Roland and Norma; Kathy; Margie and Terry; Carol and Jim; and Tom and Erica.

Five-Minute Sunday School Activities: Exploring the Bible
©2014 by Mary J. Davis

RoseKidz®
An imprint of Rose Publishing, Inc.®
17909 Adria Maru Lane
Carson, CA 90746
www.Rose-Publishing.com

Register your book at www.Rose-Publishing.com/register and receive a free Bible Reference download.

Cover Illustrator: Todd Marsh
Interior Illustrator: Chuck Galey

ISBN 10: 1-58411-048-1
ISBN 13: 978-1-58411-048-4
RoseKidz® reorder# R38421
RELIGION/Christian Ministry/Children

CONTENTS

INTRODUCTION

Children need to grow up learning the foundations of the Bible. When you teach from the Bible, your children will learn what God expects from them and what He can do for them. Children who learn the basics of God's love and care will grow and mature in their walk with the Lord.

Five-Minute Sunday School Activities is designed to give teachers a quick activity that teaches an important Bible truth. Teachers are often faced with a few extra minutes after the lesson is finished. There are also times when a teacher needs a few moments to get attendance and other important things out of the way before the main lesson. Instead of wasting these minutes with non-learning play, provide a Five-Minute activity!

The activities in the book can also be used as entire lessons. Bible story references, teaching suggestions, and memory verses are included with each activity.

EXTRA TIME suggestions are given for each activity. If you have more than five minutes, extend the lesson time with the **EXTRA TIME** option.

MOSES IS SAVED
EXODUS 2:1-10

MEMORY VERSE

Then Pharaoh's daughter ...saw the basket among the reeds and sent her slave girl to get it.

~ Exodus 2:5

WHAT YOU NEED

- page 26, duplicated
- pencils

BEFORE CLASS

Duplicate a pattern page for each child.

WHAT TO DO

1. Introduce the lesson by telling the story from Exodus 2:1-10. Don't give away the meaning of Moses' name! Say, **God provided a way for someone to take care of Moses. His mother, sister and Pharaoh's daughter were all used in God's plan to take care of Moses. God uses others in His plan to care for us. Can you name some people God might use?** Suggest: doctor, police officer, firefighter, parents.
2. Distribute a puzzle page to each child.
3. Say the memory verse.
4. Say, **Use the code to fill in the blanks with the correct vowels. Then read the phrase to find out what Moses' name means. Moses' name reminds us how well God took care of him and how well he takes care of us. Let's pray now and thank God for His care.**

EXTRA TIME

Divide the class into groups of four or five. Provide some props such as baskets, dolls, robes or towels for costumes. Give the groups a few minutes to plan a play to retell the story. Let the children perform their plays for each other or another class.

C

omplete the puzzle to discover
what Moses' name means.

= a

= e

= i

= o

= u

_ dr _ w h _ m
(i)   (e)   (i)

_ _ t _ f th _
(o)(u) (o)   (e)

w _ t _ r.
(a) (e)

Then Pharaoh's daughter …saw the basket among the reeds and sent her slave girl to get it.

~ Exodus 2:5

The solution is on page 96.

CROSSING THE RED SEA
EXODUS CHAPTERS 12-13

WHAT YOU NEED

- page 28, duplicated
- crayons or markers

BEFORE CLASS

Duplicate a pattern page for each child.

WHAT TO DO

1. Introduce the lesson by telling the Bible story from Exodus chapters 12 and 13. Have the children look in their Bibles and read Exodus 12:50, 51 aloud together. Say, **The Israelites did what God told them to do. God wants us all to obey Him.**
2. Distribute a puzzle page to each child.
3. Say the memory verse.
4. Say, **Help the Israelites find their way across the Red Sea.** Have the children complete the maze. While the children work on their mazes, discuss some of the ways in which the Israelites obeyed God. Then discuss ways in which we can obey God.

EXTRA TIME

Play "The Lord Commands." Choose one child to be Moses and one to be Aaron. Have the rest of the children stand side-by-side several feet away against one wall of the room. Say, **Moses and Aaron will take turns telling what the Lord commands. You must do what the Lord commands.** However, if they don't say, "The Lord commands!" you shouldn't do that action. Choose others to be Moses and Aaron several times so each child gets a turn at commanding.

elp the Israelites find their way across the Red Sea.

The solution is on page 96.

The Lord brought the Israelites out of Egypt by their divisions.
~ Exodus 12:51

Samson and Delilah
Judges 16:4-31

MEMORY VERSE

The boy is to be...set apart to God from birth.
~ Judges 13:5

WHAT YOU NEED

- page 32, duplicated
- crayons or markers

BEFORE CLASS

Duplicate a pattern page for each child.
Make a sample craft to show the children.

WHAT TO DO

1. Introduce the lesson by telling the story of Samson and Delilah from Judges 16:4-31. Say, **God wanted Samson to be set apart so that he would serve God in a special way all his life. God wants us to be set apart, too. There are things a Christian shouldn't do, places a Christian shouldn't go and ways a Christian shouldn't act.**
2. Show the children the sample craft.
3. Distribute a pattern page to each child.
4. Say the memory verse.
5. Have the children use as many cartoon squares as they want to draw the story of Samson and Delilah. Allow the children to show the class their cartoon drawings.

EXTRA TIME

Have the children turn in their Bibles to Numbers 6:1-8. Let the children take turns reading about Nazarites, who were set apart for service to God. This will help give them an understanding of why Samson was not to cut his hair.

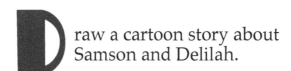raw a cartoon story about
Samson and Delilah.

Samson and Delilah

The boy is to be…set apart to God from birth.

~ Judges 13:5

RUTH PROMISES TO STAY
BOOK OF RUTH

MEMORY VERSE

Where you go, I will go, and where you stay, I will stay.

~ Ruth 1:16

WHAT YOU NEED

- page 34, duplicated
- pencils

BEFORE CLASS

Duplicate a pattern page for each child.

WHAT TO DO

1. Introduce the lesson by telling the story of Ruth from the book of Ruth. Say, **Ruth made a commitment to Naomi. A commitment is like a promise. God wants us to keep our commitments to others and do as we promise.**
2. Distribute a pattern page to each child.
3. Tell the children to put the correct letters in each blank, using the code.
4. When puzzles are finished, have the children read all of Ruth 1:16 together.
5. Have the children say the memory verse together.

EXTRA TIME

Divide the class into pairs. Talk a little about commitments, then tell the children to make a commitment with their partner.
Suggestions: Pray for each other, check on the other one if he/she misses Sunday school, be helpful, etc.

Solve the code puzzle to find out what Ruth said to Naomi.

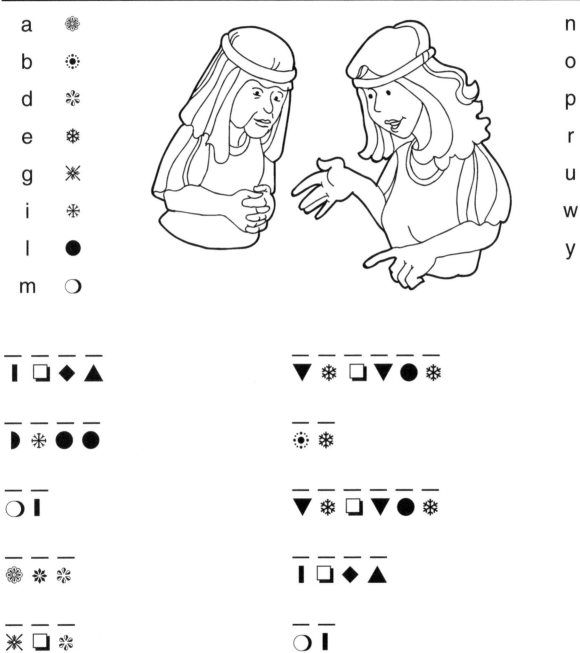

a	❀
b	☀
d	❄
e	❆
g	✻
i	✳
l	●
m	○

n	✿
o	▢
p	▼
r	▲
u	◆
w	◗
y	▮

‾▮ ‾▢ ‾◆ ‾▲

‾◗ ‾✳ ● ●

‾○ ‾▮

❀ ✿ ❄

✻ ‾▢ ❄

✻ ‾▢ ❄

‾▼ ❆ ‾▢ ‾▼ ● ❆

☀ ❆

‾▼ ❆ ‾▢ ‾▼ ● ❆

‾▮ ‾▢ ◆ ‾▲

‾○ ‾▮

The solution is on page 96.

HaNNaH keeps Her Promise
1 Samuel Chapter 1

MEMORY VERSE

I will give him to the Lord for all the days of his life.

~ 1 Samuel 1:11

WHAT YOU NEED

- page 36, duplicated
- crayons or markers

BEFORE CLASS

Duplicate a pattern page for each child.
Make a sample craft to show the children.

WHAT TO DO

1. Introduce the lesson by telling the story from 1 Samuel Chapter 11. Ask, **For what did Hannah ask God? What promise did she make to God? How did she keep her promise?**
2. Show the children the sample craft.
3. Distribute a pattern page to each child.
4. Say the memory verse.
5. Have the children fold the scene on the dashed lines, as shown.
6. Then have the children color the scenes. Discuss promises we make to God. Encourage the children to make at least one promise to God and then do their best to keep it. Suggest: pray more than once a day, invite someone to church, read the Bible, be kind to others, do something special to help keep the church clean.

EXTRA TIME

Have the children fold a plain piece of paper the same way the pattern page is folded. On the first page, have the children draw themselves praying to God.
In the center section, have the children write something for which they have prayed.
On the last section, have children draw or write how God answered their prayers.

ake a folding scene to show
what Hannah promised God,
and how she kept that promise.

I will give him to
the Lord for all the
days of his life.
~ 1 Samuel 1:11

DAVID IS ANOINTED KING
1 SAMUEL 16:1-13

MEMORY VERSE

*Man looks at the outward appearance,
but the Lord looks at the heart.*

~ 1 Samuel 16:7

WHAT YOU NEED

- page 38, duplicated
- scissors
- glue
- foil

BEFORE CLASS

Duplicate a pattern page for each child. Make a sample craft to show the children.

WHAT TO DO

1. Introduce the lesson by having the children take turns reading
   1 Samuel 16:1-13. Ask, **Did Samuel know which of Jesse's sons he was to
   anoint as king? How many sons did Jesse present to Samuel before David?
   Why do you think God looks at our hearts rather than what kind of clothes
   we wear and how nice our hair looks?**
2. Show the children the sample craft.
3. Distribute a pattern page to each child.
4. Say the memory verse.
5. Have the children cut out the crown.
6. Show how to trace the crown onto a piece of foil and cut out the foil.
7. Have the children glue the foil to the back of the crown.
8. Tell the children to look into the foil and see their image. Say, **It is not a clear
   image. But God can see a clear image of our hearts. And that is how He
   judges us: by our hearts.**

EXTRA TIME

Have the children decorate the front of the crown as they wish. Punch a hole
in the center point of the crown and thread a length of yarn through for a hanger.

ake a crown with a mirror to show that God looks at our hearts rather than what we look like outside.

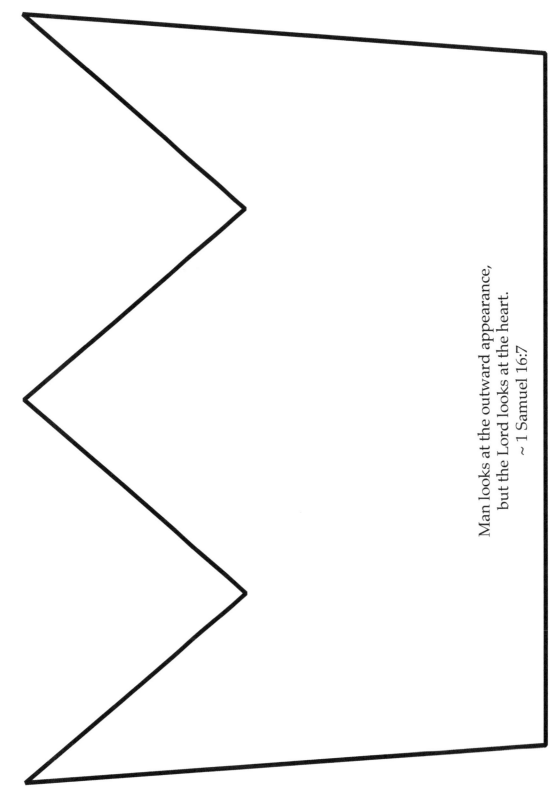

Man looks at the outward appearance, but the Lord looks at the heart. ~ 1 Samuel 16:7

DaViD anD GOLiaTH
1 Samuel Chapter 17

MEMORY VERSE

*I come against you in the
name of the Lord Almighty.*

~ 1 Samuel 17:45

WHAT YOU NEED

- page 40, duplicated
- pencils

BEFORE CLASS

Duplicate a pattern page for each
child.

WHAT TO DO

1. Introduce the lesson by telling the story of David and Goliath from 1 Samuel chapter 17. Say, **God helped David conquer Goliath. God is willing and able to help you conquer giants in your life today.**
2. Distribute a pattern page to each child.
3. Say the memory verse.
4. Tell the children to unscramble the words to discover some "giants" God helps us conquer today. Assist the children with figuring out the words if they need help. Hints are provided.

EXTRA TIME

Give each child a large sheet of construction paper and provide markers or crayons. Have the children write a newspaper story about David conquering Goliath. Encourage them to use the memory verse in their stories.

God helped David conquer a giant.
What giants can He help you conquer?
Unscramble the words below to find out.

erfa _____
(being afraid)

ederg _____
(wanting everything for yourself)

thea _____
(the opposite of love)

hisdnostey _____
(not honest)

tcihngae _____
(not doing what is honest)

lsfiesh _____
(not wanting to share with others)

ins _____
(when you do wrong, you commit this)

sleta _____
(when you take something that is not yours)

nlygi _____
(not telling the truth)

orwpshi diols _____   _____
(worshiping something besides God)

The solution is on page 96.

SOLOMON Receives a Gift
1 KINGS 3:4-15

MEMORY VERSE

I will give you a wise and discerning heart, so that there will never have been anyone like you, nor will there ever be.

~ 1 Kings 3:12

WHAT YOU NEED

- page 42, duplicated
- crayons or markers

BEFORE CLASS

Duplicate a pattern page for each child.

WHAT TO DO

1. Introduce the lesson by telling the story of Solomon from 1 Kings 3:4-15. Say, **King Solomon showed his love for God in two ways. Verse 3 says that he walked in the ways of God. In verse 9, he asks for God's help in governing the people. He asked God to help him know right from wrong. God was pleased because Solomon showed his love for God in everything he did. God is pleased when we show our love for Him by following His ways and learning to do right.**
2. Distribute a pattern page to each child.
3. Say the memory verse.
4. Tell the children to color the spaces that have a crown. Ask, **What word is revealed?**
5. Discuss what this word means. Ask, **Why would Solomon want wisdom?**
6. Ask, **How can we use wisdom to live for God today?** Suggest: know right from wrong, choose good friends, find ways to serve God and others.

EXTRA TIME

Before class, place small Bibles in a box with a lid. (Have enough small Bibles for each child to take one home.) Wrap the box as a gift. During class, pass the box around to the children. Have them try to guess what's inside. Give hints: "a gift from God," "something that gives wisdom," "teaches us," "we should use it every day." Then let the children unwrap the box to discover the Bibles. Give each child one to take home.

Find what Solomon asked for and received from God.

I will give you a wise and discerning heart, so that there will never have been anyone like you, nor will there ever be.

~ 1 Kings 3:12

42

SOLOMON BUILDS A TEMPLE
1 KINGS CHAPTER 6-8

MEMORY VERSE

I have indeed built a magnificent temple for you, a place for you to dwell forever.

~ 1 Kings 8:13

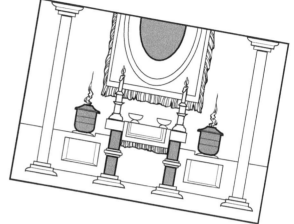

WHAT YOU NEED

- page 44, duplicated
- crayons or markers
- scissors
- glue or tape
- gold paper or yellow construction paper

BEFORE CLASS

Duplicate a pattern page for each child. Make a sample craft to show the children.

WHAT TO DO

1. Introduce the lesson by telling the story of Solomon building God's temple from 1 Kings chapters 6-8. Say, **Not every town had a church during Bible times. So God instructed His people to build a tabernacle, like a large tent, that could be moved. Then God wanted the people to build a permanent place of worship. Let's read 1 Kings 6:11-13 to see what God said to Solomon about building the temple.**
2. Show the children the sample craft.
3. Distribute a pattern page to each child.
4. Say the memory verse.
5. Have the children cut out the areas outlined in bold lines.
6. Allow the students to glue the page onto the gold or yellow paper.
7. Let the children color the poster as time allows. Say, **God still lives in His house, today. Why is God pleased that we have churches?**
   Suggest: So we will gather with other Christians, so we will go to worship Him.

EXTRA TIME

Add more sparkle to the poster by having the children glue gold and silver glitter to the outlines of the temple fixtures. The temple had many gold chains adorning the fixtures. The children may draw chains with a pencil, then outline them with glue and glitter. Pillars were bronze, so a bronze crayon or bronze glitter can be used to decorate the pillars.

43

 Make a temple poster to show the beautiful Temple Solomon built for God.

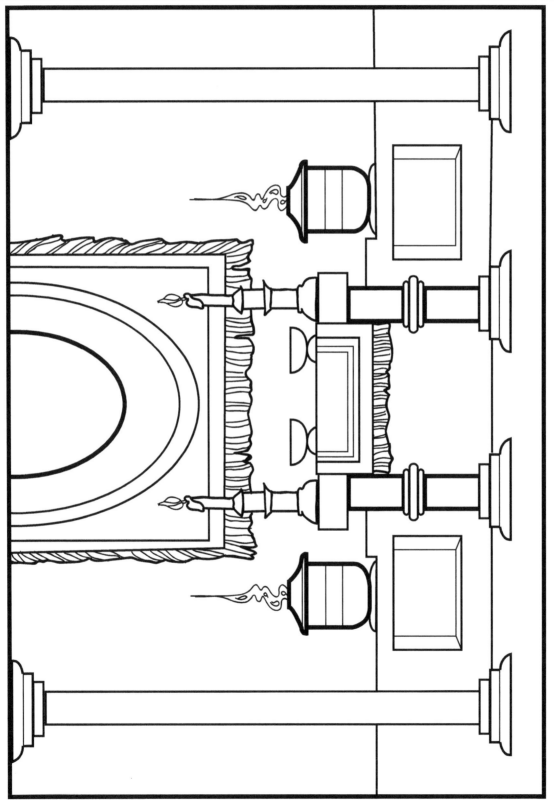

I have indeed built a magnificent temple for you, a place for you to dwell forever.
~ 1 Kings 8:13

GOD SENDS FOOD TO ELIJAH
1 KINGS 17:1-6

MEMORY VERSE

The ravens brought him bread and meat in the morning and bread and meat in the evening, and he drank from the brook.

~ 1 Kings 17:6

WHAT YOU NEED

- page 46, duplicated
- crayons or markers
- scissors
- tape
- toilet tissue tubes
- yarn

BEFORE CLASS

Duplicate a pattern page for each child. You will need about two yards of yarn per child. Make a sample craft to show the children.

WHAT TO DO

1. Introduce the lesson by telling the story from 1 Kings 17:1-6. Ask, **What is unusual about the way God provided Elijah with food? What are some unusual ways God has provided for you?**
2. Show the children the sample craft.
3. Distribute a pattern page to each child.
4. Say the memory verse.
5. Have the children cut out the raven.
6. The children may color the raven as time allows.
7. Have the children place the tissue tube at the center of the inside of the raven. They should tape the tube into place.
8. Give each child a length of yarn to thread through the tube. While the children are playing with their raven crafts, remind them that God blesses us each day. Encourage the children to name some ways God has blessed them.
9. Show how to hold one end of the yarn in each hand and "fly" the raven.

EXTRA TIME

Provide longer lengths of yarn, or some clothesline, for each pair of children. Have the children race their ravens against each other in pairs.

God sent ravens to bring food to Elijah. Make a flying raven to remember how God provided food for Elijah.

The ravens brought him bread and meat in the morning and bread and meat in the evening, and he drank from the brook.
~ 1 Kings 17:6

ELiJaH is Taken to Heaven
2 KINGS 2:1-12

MEMORY VERSE

Suddenly a chariot of fire and horses of fire appeared and separated the two of them, and Elijah went up to heaven in a whirlwind.

~ 2 Kings 2:11

WHAT YOU NEED

- page 48, duplicated
- juice cans
- scissors
- tape
- crayons or markers

BEFORE CLASS

Duplicate a pattern page for each child. Cut a 10-inch length of yarn for each child. Make a sample craft to show the children.

WHAT TO DO

1. Introduce the lesson by telling the story from 2 Kings 2:1-12. Say, **God planned that Elijah would go to heaven in a chariot of fire rather than die. God let Elisha see Elijah taken to heaven so Elisha would know he could do great things with God's help. God has a plan for each of us, too.**
2. Show the children the sample craft.
3. Distribute a pattern page to each child and say the memory verse.
4. Have the children cut out the chariot and color it with markers or crayons.
5. Have the children fold the bottom of the chariot downward.
6. Show how to set a juice can inside the chariot, and how to tape where indicated to shape the chariot and hold the juice can in place.
7. Instruct the students to tape or glue a length of yarn, around 10 inches long, to the front of the chariot.
8. Have the children color the pictures as time allows.

EXTRA TIME

Provide a large box with one side cut off; red, orange and yellow tissue paper; plain paper; markers and glue. Have the children tear "flames" from the tissue paper and glue them onto the outside of the box to make a chariot. Have each child write his or her name on the outside of the box after it is decorated. Keep the chariot on display in your classroom to remind the children that God has a special plan for everyone.

 ake a chariot to remember that God took Elijah to heaven in a chariot of fire.

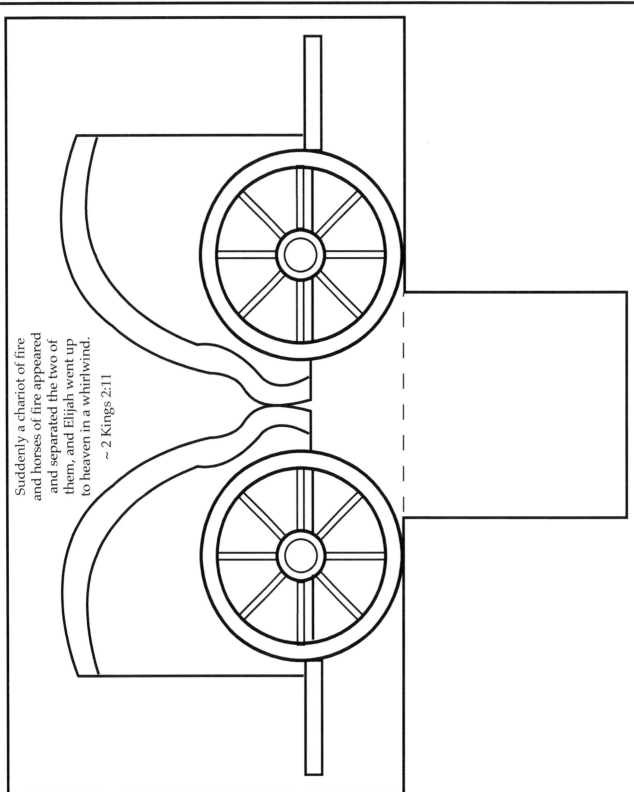

Suddenly a chariot of fire and horses of fire appeared and separated the two of them, and Elijah went up to heaven in a whirlwind.

~ 2 Kings 2:11

ELiSHa FeeDS 100 MeN
2 KiNGS 4:42-44

MEMORY VERSE

This is what the Lord says: "They will eat and have some left over."

~ 2 Kings 4:43

WHAT YOU NEED

- page 50, duplicated
- crayons or markers

BEFORE CLASS

Duplicate a pattern page for each child.

WHAT TO DO

1. Introduce the lesson by telling the story from 2 Kings 4:42-44. Say, **Remember the stories from the New Testament about Jesus feeding the 5,000 and the 4,000 with only a little food? This Old Testament story tells about Elisha feeding 100 men with a few loaves of bread.**
2. Distribute a pattern page to each child.
3. Say the memory verse. Have the children write the memory verse at the bottom of the picture. Allow time for the children to color the picture.
4. Tell the children to find and circle 20 loaves of bread.

EXTRA TIME

Place some small crackers on a plate, enough for only half the class. Pass the plate around until the crackers are gone. Then place a few more crackers on the plate. Continue until each child has at least one cracker. Say, **You saw me put more food on the plate. God, provided enough food for 100 men with only 20 loaves of bread. It was a miracle that God made the food last until everyone had enough to eat.**

R

emember the story of Jesus feeding the 5,000? This is a similar story from the Old Testament. Elisha fed 100 men with only 20 loaves of bread.

The solution is on page 96.

This is what the Lord says: "They will eat and have some left over."
~ 2 Kings 4:43

Naaman is Healed
2 Kings 5:1-14

MEMORY VERSE

So he went down and dipped himself in the Jordan seven times, as the man of God had told him, and his flesh was restored.

~ 2 Kings 5:14

WHAT YOU NEED

- page 52, duplicated
- pencils
- crayons or markers

BEFORE CLASS

Duplicate a puzzle for each child.
Note: The puzzle will be easier for older students, but all will be reminded of the number of times Naaman had to dip before he was healed.

WHAT TO DO

1. Introduce the lesson by having the children take turns reading 2 Kings 5:1-14. Say, **Naaman was angry at first. He didn't want to go into the Jordan River. There were other rivers that were cleaner and nicer. In fact, Naaman wanted to know why God didn't just "zap" him to make him well. But God wanted Naaman to learn to obey.**
2. Distribute a puzzle page to each child and say the memory verse.
3. Explain to the children that they should look at each scrambled word. They should decide what each word spells, then write the corresponding number in the blank next to the word. (The words spell the numbers from one to seven.)
4. Remind the children that Naaman dipped seven times in the Jordan. Say, **If Naaman had not followed God's directions, he would not have been healed. It is important for us to follow God's directions in our lives, too.**
5. Allow the children to color the picture as time permits.

EXTRA TIME

Provide a large piece of newsprint. Have seven children or groups of children draw Naaman dipping in the Jordan River and have them number the pictures from one to seven. If you have a large group, make more than one mural so every child gets to participate in the drawings.

Do the puzzle as a reminder of how many times God told Naaman to dip in the water before He healed him.

RUFO _____   WOT _____

                                    VENSE _____

IXS _____

VFEI _____

                              NEO _____

ETERH _____

52

JOB PRAISES GOD
JOB CHAPTERS 1, 2 & 42

MEMORY VERSE

*[Job] was blameless and upright;
he feared God and shunned evil.*

~ Job 1:1

WHAT YOU NEED

- page 54, duplicated
- crayons or markers
- scissors
- tape
- craft sticks

BEFORE CLASS

Duplicate a pattern page for each child. Make a sample craft to show the children.

WHAT TO DO

1. Introduce the lesson by telling the story from Job chapters 1, 2 and 42. Say, **God doesn't always keep troubles away from us. But He always helps us through our troubles. Sometimes bad times can teach us to put our trustin God.**
2. Show the children the sample craft.
3. Distribute a pattern page to each child.
4. Say the memory verse.
5. Have the children cut out the six puppets.
6. Show how to tape a craft stick to the bottom edge of each puppet. While the children work, talk about the memory verse. Say, **Job was blameless, meaning he tried his best to please God. He feared God, which means he obeyed God's Word the best he could. He shunned evil, which means he turned away from sin. These are all things we can do, too.**

EXTRA TIME

Provide large sheets of construction paper. Have the children fold the page in half so it stands up. They can draw a scene on one or both sides of the paper and use them as scenes for the puppets.

ake puppets to tell Job's story.

Job

Job's wife

Eliphaz

Zophar

Bildad

Elihu

THREE MEN IN A FIERY FURNACE
DANIEL CHAPTER 3

MEMORY VERSE

Praise be to the God of Shadrach, Meshach and Abednego, who has sent his angel and rescued his servants!

~ Daniel 3:28

WHAT YOU NEED

- page 56, duplicated
- crayons or markers

BEFORE CLASS

Duplicate a pattern page for each child.

WHAT TO DO

1. Introduce the lesson by telling the story from Daniel chapter 3. Say, **This is one of the true stories in the Bible that teaches us God will keep us safe when we are persecuted for our beliefs. "Persecuted" means that someone is trying to stop us from worshiping God or believing in Him.**
2. Distribute a pattern page to each child.
3. Say the memory verse.
4. Have the children connect the dots to find Shadrach, Meshach and Abednego.
5. Then have the children shade in the shapes with a flame to see who else is in the furnace. When the children discover Jesus in the picture, discuss times when Jesus helps each of us.

EXTRA TIME

Provide plain paper and crayons or markers, and pencils. Have the children write or draw about a time when they knew Jesus was helping them.

ow many men were in the furnace?
Complete the picture and find out.

Praise be to the God of Shadrach, Meshach and Abednego,
who has sent his angel and rescued his servants!
~ Daniel 3:28

The solution is on page 96.

DANIEL IN THE LIONS' DEN
DANIEL CHAPTER 6

MEMORY VERSE

For he is the living God and he endures forever; his kingdom will not be destroyed, his dominion will never end.

~ Daniel 6:26

WHAT YOU NEED

- pages 58 and 59, duplicated
- heavy white paper or card stock
- crayons or markers
- scissors

BEFORE CLASS

Duplicate the pattern pages onto heavy white paper or card stock for each child. Make a sample craft to show the children.

WHAT TO DO

1. Introduce the lesson by having the children read the story from Daniel, chapter 6. Say, **Daniel prayed to God, even when others tried to stop him. God wants us to always worship and pray. He will help us when someone tries to keep us from doing so.**
2. Show the children the sample craft.
3. Distribute both pattern pages to each child.
4. Say the memory verse.
5. Have the children cut out the four figures.
6. Show how to fold the figures on the dashed lines and stand them up.
7. Allow the children to color the figures as time allows. As the children work, discuss situations in which someone might try to stop us from praying or worshiping God in some way.

EXTRA TIME

Have the children each write out a pledge to help the others in the class to continue in prayer and worship. Keep the pledges in a folder in the classroom, or post them on a bulletin board. Say, **When someone or something tempts you to stop praying or worshiping God, ask your friends in the class to help you continue to do right. Let's pray for each other that we all continue to worship God regularly.**

ake stand up figures to tell the
story of Daniel in the lions' den.

For he is the living God
and he endures forever;
his kingdom will not be
destroyed, his dominion
will never end.

~ Daniel 6:26

59

JONAH IS SWALLOWED
JONAH CHAPTERS 1 & 2

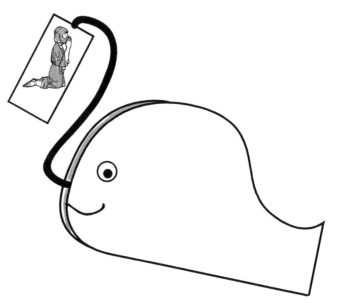

MEMORY VERSE

The Lord provided a great fish to swallow Jonah, and Jonah was inside the fish three days and three nights.

~ Jonah 1:17

WHAT YOU NEED

- page 61, duplicated
- crayons or markers
- scissors
- tape
- yarn
- paper plates

BEFORE CLASS

Duplicate a pattern page for each child. Make a sample craft to show the children.

WHAT TO DO

1. Introduce the lesson by telling the story of Jonah from the book of Jonah, chapters 1 and 2. Say, **Jonah tried to run from God. He didn't want to do what God said. God wants us to obey Him, too. He will help us do what He says.**
2. Show the children the sample craft.
3. Distribute a pattern page to each child, and say the memory verse.
4. Have the children cut out the two fish figures and the Jonah double figure.
5. Instruct the children to fold the plate in half and tape it closed at the midway point of the curved side. They should tape a fish on each side of the folded plate.
6. Help the children cut a length of yarn about two feet long. They should tape one end of the yarn inside Jonah, and the other end inside the fish's mouth.
7. Let the children use the remaining class time to act out the story using the big fish and Jonah figures.
8. Discuss some things God wants us to do. Encourage the children to name some ways God will help us do good things for Him. Suggest: Tell others about God, do a job at church that seems to be too big, pray out loud in a group.

EXTRA TIME

Make a ship by folding a second plate in half and taping it at the top. Have the children decorate the ship. Instead of using yarn, keep the Jonah figure free. Move Jonah from the ship to the fish.

Jonah ran from God. But God still saved Jonah from drowning by sending a big fish to swallow him. Jonah prayed and repented. God had the fish spit Jonah onto the shore.

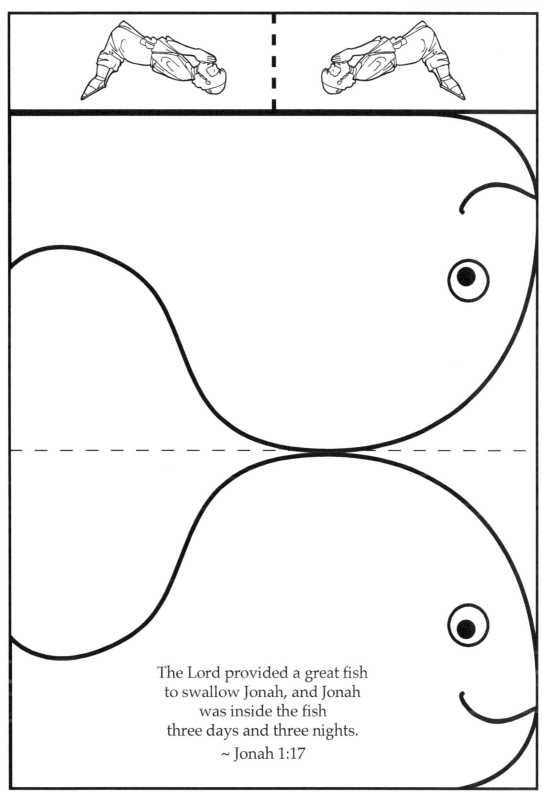

The Lord provided a great fish
to swallow Jonah, and Jonah
was inside the fish
three days and three nights.

~ Jonah 1:17

JESUS IS BORN
LUKE 2:1-7

MEMORY VERSE

She wrapped him in cloths and placed him in a manger, because there was no room for them in the inn.

~ Luke 2:7

WHAT YOU NEED

- page 63, duplicated
- crayons or markers
- scissors
- tape
- yarn
- hole punch

BEFORE CLASS

Duplicate a pattern page for each child. Make a sample craft to show the children.

WHAT TO DO

1. Introduce the lesson by having the children take turns reading aloud the story from Luke 2:1-7. Say, **This story of Jesus' birth is a wonderful story to read and remember any time of the year, not just at Christmas. Jesus was born for a purpose. He was sent to us by God so we would have a wonderful Savior.**
2. Show the children the sample craft.
3. Distribute a pattern page to each child.
4. Say the memory verse.
5. Have the children cut the bookmark from the page and fold it on the dashed line.
6. They should tape the edge of the bookmark to hold it together.
7. The children may color the bookmark as time allows. Then have them punch several holes around the folded bookmark.
8. Give each child a length of yarn around 3 feet long. Help the children tape one end of the yarn beside one of the holes.
9. Have the children lace the yarn through the holes. Show how to tape the yarn to the bookmark after the last hole. Cut off any excess yarn.

EXTRA TIME

Have the children make extra bookmarks to give to another class as gifts.

Make a lace-up bookmark to mark the story of Jesus' birth in your Bible.

She wrapped him in cloths and placed him in a manger, because there was no room for them in the inn.

Luke 2:7

ANGELS BRING GOOD NEWS
LUKE 2:8-20

But the angel said to them, "Do not be afraid. I bring you good news of great joy that will be for all the people."
~ Luke 2:10

WHAT YOU NEED

- page 65, duplicated
- crayons or markers
- scissors
- tape or glue
- plastic butter dishes, 1-lb. size
- candy or other treats

BEFORE CLASS

Duplicate a pattern page for each child. You will need one plastic butter dish for each child. Bring extra candy or treats for snacking.

WHAT TO DO

1. Introduce the lesson by telling the story from Luke 2:8-20. Say, **Can you imagine how bright and beautiful the sky became when all the angels appeared? Can you imagine the beautiful sound all those angels made when they praised God? We are going to make an angel candy dish. The angels will remind us to praise God for Jesus.**
2. Show the children the sample craft.
3. Distribute a pattern page to each child, and say the memory verse.
4. Have the children cut the four squares from the page.
5. Allow them to color the angel pictures with crayons or markers.
6. Show how to tape or glue the angel squares around the outside of a butter dish.
7. Give the children some candy or treats to put in their candy dishes to take home.
8. Say, **We should praise God for sending Jesus as our Savior!**

EXTRA TIME

Provide extra materials and treats. Have the children make angel dishes to distribute at a nursing home. Provide plastic wrap to cover the bowls to keep the contents from falling out.

Angels told the shepherds in the fields about Jesus' birth. Make an angel dish to share the Good News.

But the angel said to them, "Do not be afraid. I bring you good news of great joy that will be for all the people."

~ Luke 2:10

But the angel said to them, "Do not be afraid. I bring you good news of great joy that will be for all the people."

~ Luke 2:10

But the angel said to them, "Do not be afraid. I bring you good news of great joy that will be for all the people."

~ Luke 2:10

But the angel said to them, "Do not be afraid. I bring you good news of great joy that will be for all the people."

~ Luke 2:10

MAGI BRING GIFTS TO JESUS
MATTHEW 2:1-12

MEMORY VERSE

*They bowed down and worshiped him.
Then they opened their treasures
and presented him with gifts.*

~ Matthew 2:11

WHAT YOU NEED

- page 67, duplicated
- pencils

BEFORE CLASS

Duplicate a pattern page for each child.

WHAT TO DO

1. Introduce the lesson by telling the children the story from Matthew 2:1-12. Say, **The magi knew Jesus was God's Son. They brought gifts to honor the Son of God. We can give gifts to honor Jesus, too. Who can tell a gift we can give?** Suggest: Our praises, serving Him, giving food to help others, cleaning the church building, giving money in the offering.
2. Distribute a pattern page to each child.
3. Say the memory verse.
4. Tell the children to solve the "opposite" riddles to fill in the blanks.
5. Have the children color the treasure chests as time allows. Say, **The magi gave treasures to Jesus. We can give Him treasures, too.**

EXTRA TIME

Plan a project the class can do together to honor Jesus. Let the children help decide on the project. If the project can be done immediately, work together to complete it during class time. If the project takes more time or some materials, decide on a good time. Get parents involved if necessary.

Wise Men Worship Jesus
Matthew 2:1-12

The Wise Men traveled to Jerusalem to find baby Jesus.

The Wise Men followed a star.

The star stopped over the house where Jesus was with His parents.

The Wise Men gave Jesus gifts.

MEMORY VERSE

We saw his star in the east and have come to worship him.
~ Matthew 2:2

WHAT YOU NEED

- page 62, duplicated
- crayons
- glue
- glitter

BEFORE CLASS

Duplicate a pattern page for each child. Make a sample craft to show the children.

WHAT TO DO

1. Introduce the lesson by telling the story from Matthew 2:1-12. Say, **The wise men searched for baby Jesus. They followed the star to find Him. We are happy, too, that Jesus was born. We can worship Jesus like the wise men did.**
2. Show the children the sample craft.
3. Distribute a pattern page to each child.
4. Say the memory verse.
5. Have the children spread glue around the edge of the star, then sprinkle on glitter.
6. Allow the students to color the picture.
7. Read each section of the poster before the children color. Prepare the children to be able to retell the story at home.

EXTRA TIME

Cut out at least one small star shape from construction paper for each child. Let the children add stickers of baby Jesus to the stars. Add a length of yarn for a hanger. Say, **We can hang our stars on our Christmas trees at home to remember to worship Jesus.**

ake a poster to tell about the
Wise Men following a star to
find baby Jesus.

The Wise Men traveled to
Jerusalem to find baby Jesus.

The Wise Men followed a star.

The star stopped over the house
where Jesus was with His parents.

The Wise Men gave Jesus gifts.

Solve the puzzle to find what gifts the Magi gave to Jesus.

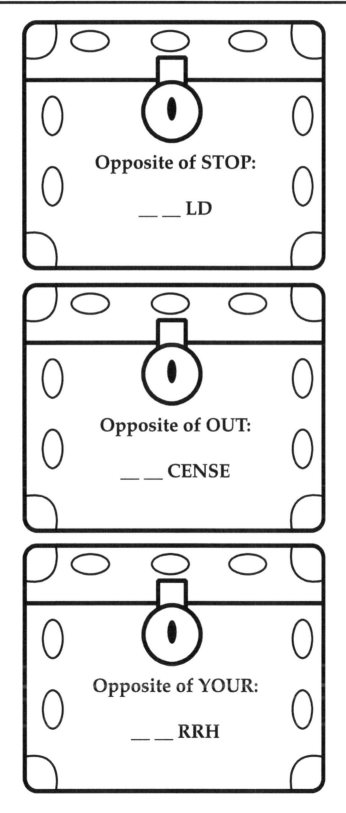

Opposite of STOP:

_ _ LD

Opposite of OUT:

_ _ CENSE

Opposite of YOUR:

_ _ RRH

The solution is on page 96.

JOHN THE BAPTIST IS BORN
LUKE 1:5-25, 57-80

WHAT YOU NEED

- page 69, duplicated
- crayons or markers
- scissors
- paper fasteners

BEFORE CLASS

Duplicate a pattern page for each child. Make a sample craft to show the children.

WHAT TO DO

1. Introduce the lesson by telling the story from Luke 1:5-25, 57-80. Say, **Sometimes we doubt that God can do what He promises. God always has a reason for what He promises. John grew up and led many people back to God. When we doubt, God doesn't close our mouths, like he did Zechariah. But He gave us this true story to help us know He always keeps His promises.**
2. Show the children the sample craft.
3. Distribute a pattern page to each child, and say the memory verse.
4. Have the children cut the square and the circle from the page.
5. Show how to cut out the mouth opening.
6. Have the children color the three mouths on the circle.
7. Show how to push a paper fastener through the face and the mouth circle at the Xs. Cover the prongs with tape to avoid injury.
8. Have the children move the mouth circle so that the three different mouths show. Encourage the children to tell of a time when they, too, doubted God. Let them color the face as time allows.

EXTRA TIME

Play Doubt or Dare. Write short activities on slips of paper. Put the papers in a bowl. Have the children take turns drawing out a slip of paper. The child should read the phrase aloud and the class should guess, doubt or dare. If the person can do the suggested activity, he or she gets a small treat or prize. Say, **We can guess at whether each person can do something, but we know God always does what He says.**

ake a moving picture to show that Zechariah's mouth was closed because he did not believe Elizabeth would have a baby.

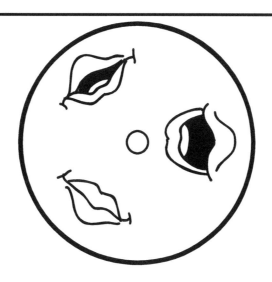

Many of the people of Israel will he bring back to the Lord their God.
~ Luke 1:16

JOHN PREPARES THE WAY
MATTHEW 3:1-12

MEMORY VERSE

*Prepare the way for the Lord,
make straight paths for him.*

~ Matthew 3:3

 WHAT YOU NEED

- page 71, duplicated
- crayons, markers or pencils

 BEFORE CLASS

Duplicate a pattern page for each child.

WHAT TO DO

1. Introduce the lesson by having the children take turns reading Matthew 3:1-12.
   Say, **God sent John to tell the people a Savior was coming. He even called
   him "the Lord." Many people understood they needed to stop sinning to
   get ready for Jesus. We don't have to wait for the Savior to come.
   But we do need to try not to sin and work hard at living for God.**
2. Distribute a pattern page to each child.
3. Say the memory verse.
4. Tell the children to find their way through the maze to Jesus.
5. After all the students have finished, have a volunteer read the verse that is in
   the correct path. Discuss ways we can keep our paths straight for the Lord.
   Suggest: go to church, pray, read our Bibles, do what is right.

 EXTRA TIME

Make two or three simple mazes in the classroom or an outdoor area. To make
the mazes, tape toilet tissue to the floor in a maze pattern. The patterns may cross
each other, but make sure one path is straight. The others should be crooked and
impossible to follow, such as running into a wall or a tree, into a trash can, etc.
At the end of the straight path, place a picture of Jesus. Let the children try to follow
the mazes. Say, **The best path to follow is the path that leads straight to Jesus.**

ollow the path to Jesus. Why do we not want to follow a crooked path? Read the words in the correct path through the maze.

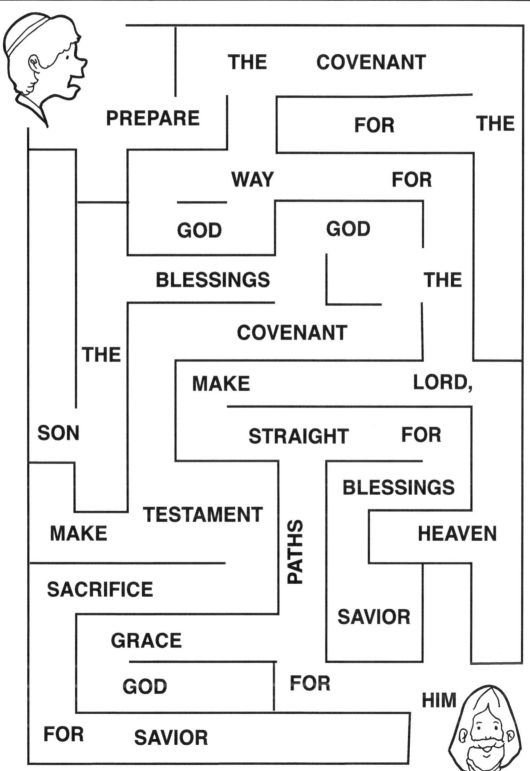

THE   COVENANT

PREPARE

FOR   THE

WAY   FOR

GOD   GOD

BLESSINGS   THE

COVENANT

THE

MAKE   LORD,

SON

STRAIGHT   FOR

BLESSINGS

TESTAMENT

PATHS   HEAVEN

MAKE

SACRIFICE

SAVIOR

GRACE

GOD   FOR

HIM

FOR   SAVIOR

The solution is on page 96.

JOHN BAPTIZES JESUS
MATTHEW 3:13-17

MEMORY VERSE

At that moment heaven was opened, and he saw the Spirit of God descending like a dove and lighting on him.
~ Matthew 3:16

WHAT YOU NEED

- page 73, duplicated
- crayons or markers
- scissors
- tape

BEFORE CLASS

Duplicate a pattern page for each child. Make a sample craft to show the children.

WHAT TO DO

1. Introduce the lesson by having the children take turns reading the story from Matthew 3:13-17. Say, **How do you feel when you hear your parent say, "This is my son/daughter? I am so proud of him/her?" Or maybe your mom or dad says to you, "I love you!" This is what God wanted the world to know about Jesus: "This is My Son, I love Him and I'm proud of Him."**
2. Show the children the sample craft.
3. Distribute a pattern page to each child, and say the memory verse.
4. Have the children cut out the scene and the two strips.
5. Help the students cut the two slits in the scene.
6. Have the children tape the two strips into a long strip.
7. Show how to thread the strip through the slits, making sure the writing is visible.
8. Have the students tape the strip together at the back to form a round strip.
9. Let the children color the scene as time allows. Remind the children that Jesus was God's Son. Let the children tell some stories about Jesus that they know. Say, **God sent Jesus to do these things. God was very proud of His Son. He is very proud of us when we serve Him, too.**

EXTRA TIME

Play a version of Pin the Tail on the Donkey. Duplicate and enlarge the scene part of the craft. Tape the scene of Jesus onto a large piece of newsprint or poster board. Fasten the game to the wall. Give each child a white dove sticker or a dove cut from white paper (add a loop of tape to the back of the cutouts). Have the children take turns being blindfolded and trying to put the dove above Jesus' head.

 ake a scrolling story picture to tell what God said about Jesus.

_____

_____

At that moment heaven was opened, and he saw the Spirit of God descending like a

and lighting on him.

Matthew 3:16

JESUS IS TEMPTED
MATTHEW 4:1-17

MEMORY VERSE

It is written: "Worship the Lord your God, and serve him only."

~ Matthew 4:10

WHAT YOU NEED

- page 75, duplicated
- crayons or markers
- tape

BEFORE CLASS

Duplicate a pattern page for each child.
Make a sample craft to show the children.

WHAT TO DO

1. Introduce the lesson by telling the story of Jesus' temptation from Matthew 4:1-17. Say, **Jesus was tempted by the devil. Jesus answered each time with a verse from God's Word. When we are tempted, we can fight off the sin by using God's Word, too.**
2. Show the children the sample craft.
3. Distribute a pattern page to each child.
4. Say the memory verse.
5. Have the children fold the page in half and tape the top and sides, leaving the bottom open.
6. Have the children color the puppets as time allows.
7. As the children work, discuss how Jesus fought off temptation, and how they can do the same.

EXTRA TIME

Have the children take turns using their puppet to tell how they allow God to help them not sin. (Many children will talk for a puppet, rather than speaking in front of the class themselves.)

 ake a double puppet to show that Jesus was tempted, just as we are tempted.

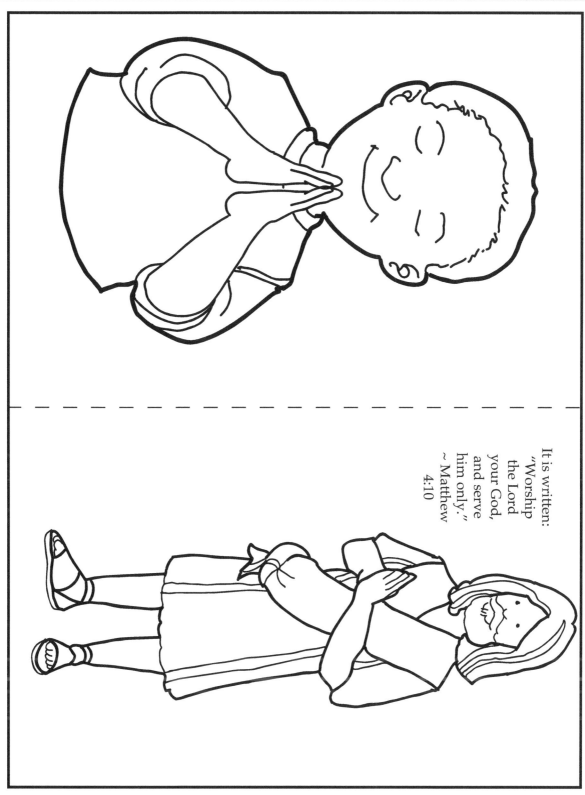

It is written: "Worship the Lord your God, and serve him only." ~ Matthew 4:10

JESUS CALLS 12 FOLLOWERS
LUKE 5:1-1, 27-32; 6:12-16; JOHN 1:35-51

MEMORY VERSE

Simon (whom he named Peter), his brother Andrew, James, John, Philip, Bartholomew, Matthew, Thomas, James son of Alphaeus, Simon who was called the Zealot, Judas son of James, and Judas Iscariot, who became a traitor.
~ Luke 6:14-16

WHAT YOU NEED

- page 77, duplicated
- crayons or markers
- scissors
- tape

BEFORE CLASS

Duplicate the pattern page for each child. Make a sample craft to show the children.

WHAT TO DO

1. Introduce the lesson by telling the story from Luke 5:1-1, 27-32; 6:12-16; and John 1:35-51. Say, **These 12 were chosen to follow Jesus, preach and teach, and heal. What kinds of things are we chosen to do for Jesus today?**
2. Show the children the sample craft.
3. Distribute a pattern page to each child.
4. Say the memory verse.
5. Have the children cut out the three bracelets on the solid lines, then fold on the dashed lines.
6. While the children color their bracelets, discuss ways we can follow Jesus today.
7. Help the children tape the bracelets around their wrists. Encourage them to give the third bracelet to a friend.

EXTRA TIME

Provide plain paper. Have the children cut strips of paper 8½" x 3½". (They can fold the paper into thirds and cut it apart to make three bracelets.) Have the children fold and decorate the bracelets as they wish, and give them to a friend. Have the children write this part of the memory verse on each bracelet: Chosen to Follow Jesus.

ake and wear some bracelets to show that you are a follower of Jesus, also.

 # Follow Me

Luke 5:1-1, 27-32; 6:12-16; John 1:35-51

 # Friend of Jesus

Luke 5:1-1, 27-32; 6:12-16; John 1:35-51

 # I am chosen

Luke 5:1-1, 27-32; 6:12-16; John 1:35-51

Zacchaeus Changes

LUKE 19:1-10

MEMORY VERSE

"I give half of my possessions to the poor, and if I have cheated anybody out of anything, I will pay back four times the amount."

~ Luke 19:8

WHAT YOU NEED

- page 79, duplicated
- pencils

BEFORE CLASS

Duplicate a pattern page for each child.

WHAT TO DO

1. Introduce the lesson by having the children read the story from Luke 19:1-10. Say, **We often look at people and say things like, "I know they did something wrong. They can't be followers of Jesus." But Jesus chose Zacchaeus to visit that day. Do you know why?** Suggest: We are all sinners. Jesus loves everyone. People change when they meet Jesus.
2. Distribute a pattern page to each child.
3. Say the memory verse.
4. Have the children open their Bibles to the story and complete the crossword puzzle. Discuss ways we can show Jesus we are changed because of knowing Him. Suggest: share with others, go to church, invite someone to church, don't gossip, be kind to everyone, obey parents.

EXTRA TIME

Have the children make simple kazoos by placing a tissue over a comb or fastening a tissue to the end of a toilet tissue tube with a rubber band.
Have them play the song "Zacchaeus" by singing or humming with their kazoos.

J esus chose to visit with Zacchaeus, who was a wealthy tax collector. He was known as a sinner. Jesus' decision to come to Zacchaeus' home was enough to change him.

Fill in the crossword puzzle. Find the answers in Luke 19:1-10.

The solution is on page 96.

<u>Down</u>
1. Whose house was Jesus going to? (verse 5)
3. What did Zacchaeus do gladly? (verse 6)
5. How many times would Zacchaeus pay back anyone he had cheated? (verse 8)
6. What town did Jesus enter? (verse 1)
7. What did Jesus say had come to Zacchaeus' house today? (verse 9)

<u>Across</u>
2. What did Zacchaeus collect? (verse 2)
4. What kind of man did the people say Zacchaeus was? (verse 7)
6. Who did Zacchaeus want to see? (verse 3)
8. What kind of tree was Zacchaeus in? (verse 4)
9. How much of his possessions did Zacchaeus say he would give to the poor? (verse 8)
10. The Son of Man came to seek and save what was __ __ __ __. (verse 10)

THE TRIUMPHAL ENTRY
MARK 11:1-11

MEMORY VERSE

Many people spread their cloaks on the road, while others spread branches they had cut in the fields.

~ Mark 11:8

WHAT YOU NEED

- page 81, duplicated
- pencils

BEFORE CLASS

Duplicate a pattern page for each child.

WHAT TO DO

1. Introduce the lesson by telling the story from Mark 11:1-11. Say, **"Hosanna" means "save." The people knew that Jesus was God's Son. The people knew a Savior was coming someday. They were sure this man, Jesus, was the Savior for whom they had been waiting.**
2. Distribute a pattern page to each child.
3. Say the memory verse.
4. Have the children search for the listed words in the puzzle. While the children work, discuss how excited the people were to see Jesus. Discuss ways we can show our love for Jesus today.

EXTRA TIME

Have a praise session. Arrange chairs in a circle. Have the children sit on the chairs and take turns standing to lead the others in favorite praise songs, prayer and even testimonies of what Jesus means to them.

See how many of these words you can find from the story of the Triumphal Entry from Mark 11:1-11 in the word search puzzle.

Jerusalem
Bethphage
Bethany
Mount of Olives
Jesus

Disciples
village
colt
untie
Lord

cloaks
branches
shouted
hosanna
blessed

The solution is on page 96.

```
A  B  H  O  S  A  N  N  A  C  D  E  F
G  J  H  I  C  L  O  A  K  S  J  S  K
S  L  E  M  N  O  P  Q  R  S  U  T  W
E  B  A  R  B  C  D  E  F  S  G  D  H
H  E  T  R  U  V  B  L  E  S  S  E  D
C  T  C  N  J  S  E  J  L  F  R  T  I
N  H  O  B  S  G  A  T  W  I  E  U  D
A  A  L  C  E  I  O  L  O  R  D  O  I
R  N  T  C  G  T  P  L  E  J  U  H  S
B  Y  D  R  A  L  H  M  N  M  C  S  C
P  O  R  T  L  F  G  P  U  Y  R  S  I
V  B  H  S  L  O  P  I  H  C  V  R  P
W  E  D  E  I  T  N  U  A  A  L  J  L
V  B  Y  P  V  F  D  T  Y  R  G  V  E
M  O  U  N  T  O  F  O  L  I  V  E  S
```

JUDAS BETRAYS JESUS

MATTHEW 26:14-16; 47-49

MEMORY VERSE

Judas watched for an opportunity to hand him over.

~ Matthew 26:16

WHAT YOU NEED

- page 83, duplicated
- pencils

BEFORE CLASS

Duplicate a pattern page for each child.

WHAT TO DO

1. Introduce the lesson by telling the story from Matthew 26:14-16, 47-49. Say, **Judas betrayed Jesus for a few coins. We sometimes betray Jesus, too. A movie or other activity may keep us from studying our Bibles or even praying. We may get too busy to go to church. We may become greedy and not want to share our food or things with someone in need.**
2. Show the children the sample craft.
3. Distribute a pattern page to each child.
4. Say the memory verse.
5. Tell the children to open their Bibles and find Matthew 26:48-49. Say, **Judas watched for the right time to betray Jesus. Sometimes we betray Him without thinking. Let's pray together and ask God to help us not to betray Him.**
6. Have the children write one word from the verse in each coin.

EXTRA TIME

Make a game with the page. Have the children glue their page to a piece of construction paper. Provide a plastic bag or letter-size envelope with at least 10 pieces of popcorn, macaroni, beans, pennies or pebbles. To play the game, a child should place the page on the floor and stand back a few feet. The child should toss 10 pennies (or another item) onto the game page. Then the child should count to see how many pennies (or items) landed in the circles. This game may be played with one or several children.

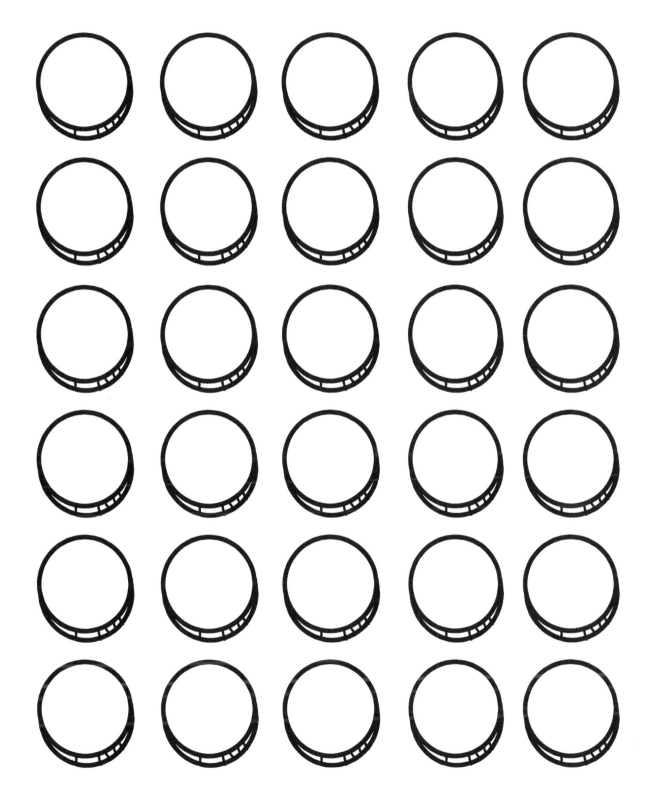

Fill in the coins to form the verses
that tell how Judas betrayed Jesus.

JESUS IS CRUCIFIED
MATTHEW 27:32-61

MEMORY VERSE

Surely he was the Son of God!
~ Matthew 27:54

WHAT YOU NEED

- page 85, duplicated
- crayons or markers
- construction paper
- scissors
- glue

BEFORE CLASS

Duplicate a pattern page for each child. Make a sample craft to show the children.

WHAT TO DO

1. Introduce the lesson by telling the story from Matthew 27:32-61. Say, **It doesn't seem fair that Jesus died, does it? It seems that the leaders of that day should have let Jesus go free. But it was God's plan that Jesus would die on the cross. God planned this so that all of us can have everlasting life in heaven.**
2. Show the children the sample craft.
3. Distribute a pattern page to each child.
4. Say the memory verse.
5. Have the children decorate the poster with crayons or markers.
6. Make a framed picture. Trim the poster about 1 inch all around. Then show how to glue the poster to a sheet of construction paper. Cut each corner of the construction paper at an angle to the poster. Fold and tape each corner.
7. When the posters are finished, have the children take turns reading the poem.

EXTRA TIME

Distribute plain paper or construction paper to the children. Tell the children they may draw a cross on the paper, then write a poem or prayer to thank God for sending us a Savior.

Decorate a poem poster to remember that Jesus' death was God's plan for the world.

Jesus was arrested,
It was God's plan,
For Jesus to be given
Into the hands of man.

Jesus was put on trial
Before rulers of that day.
And though Jesus did no wrong,
God planned it to happen that way.

Then Jesus was led away,
Up to Golgotha's hill.
Then Jesus was hung upon a cross,
Yes, even this was God's will.

There really was a reason.
God had a perfect plan.
For Jesus died upon the cross
To save every child, woman
and man.

HE IS RISEN!
MARK 16:1-14

MEMORY VERSE

He has risen! He is not here.

~ Mark 16:6

WHAT YOU NEED

- page 87, duplicated
- pencils, crayons or markers

BEFORE CLASS

Duplicate a pattern page for each child.

WHAT TO DO

1. Introduce the lesson by telling the story from Mark 16:1-14. Say,
   **Although Jesus died and was put in a tomb, He rose, just as He had said.
   Not only does this prove to us that Jesus is truly our Savior and God's Son,
   it also gives us the promise that we, too, will have eternal life.**
2. Distribute a pattern page to each child.
3. Tell the children to use the code letters to solve the puzzle.
4. Say the memory verse.

EXTRA TIME

Before class, write the memory verse on several pieces of paper. Hide the papers around the room. Tell the children they are going to play a riddle game. Explain that if they find all the papers, they will discover something special. After all the papers have been retrieved, gather the children together. Say, **The answer to the riddle is our memory verse. Let's say it together.**

Solve the puzzle to find what the man in the white robe said to the women.

---

a= ✝   i= (helmet)   r= (woman)

e= (bread)   n= (jar)   s= (flower)

h= (dove)   o= (mountains)   t= (angel)

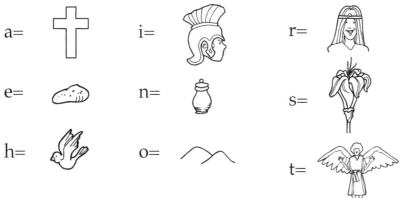

____ ____   ____ ____ ____   ____ ____ ____ ____ _____!

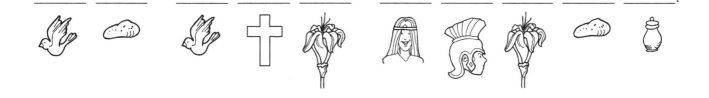

____ ____   ____ ____   ____ ____ _____

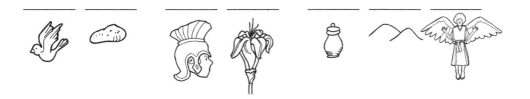

____ ____ ____ ____.   Mark 16:6

The solution is on page 96.

JESUS GiVES a COMMAND
MARK 16:14-20

WHAT YOU NEED

- page 89, duplicated
- scissors
- tape
- paper clips

BEFORE CLASS

Duplicate a game board. Copy at least one board for every four or five children. Color the game board(s), if you choose.

WHAT TO DO

1. Introduce the lesson by having the children read the story from Mark 16:14-20. Say, **Jesus was about to go to heaven to sit at God's right hand. But before He went, He gave a command to His followers. This command is meant for us today, too.**
2. Say the memory verse.
3. Place the game board on the floor and have the children stand in a line, a few feet behind the game board. (If you have a large class, divide the children into smaller groups and use more than one game board.)
4. Give each child a paper clip.
5. Have the children toss the paper clip onto the game board.
6. Let each child toss a paper clip and keep track of his or her score. Allow more than one turn if time allows. The highest score wins.
7. While the children are playing the game, have them read some of the phrases out loud. Encourage the children to suggest other ways they can "go into the world and preach the Good News."

EXTRA TIME

Have a tournament. Divide the class into groups of three or four.
Let the children each have three paper clips to toss. Keep score until everyone in each group has a turn. Then allow the winners in each group to compete together until there is one grand winner.

FIVE MINUTE

Play a fun game to remember that Jesus wants us to tell others about Him.

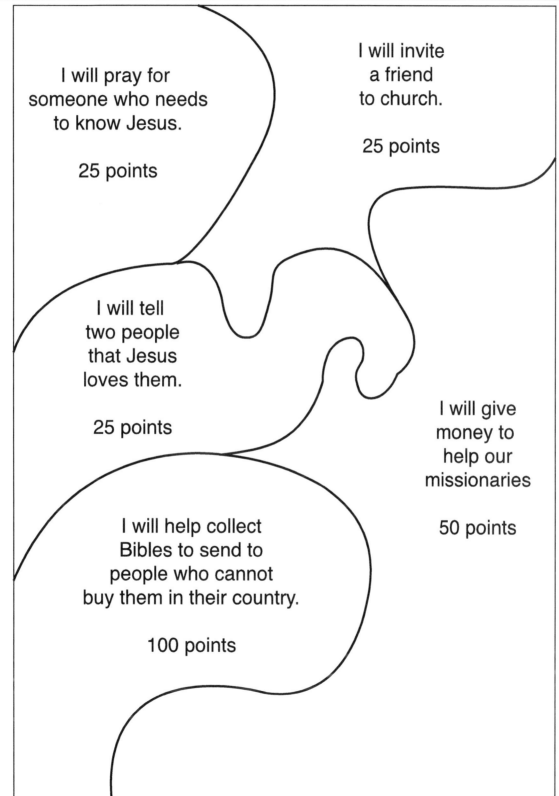

I will pray for someone who needs to know Jesus.

25 points

I will invite a friend to church.

25 points

I will tell two people that Jesus loves them.

25 points

I will give money to help our missionaries

50 points

I will help collect Bibles to send to people who cannot buy them in their country.

100 points

GOD SENDS THE HOLY SPIRIT
ACTS CHAPTER 2

MEMORY VERSE

Suddenly a sound like the blowing of a violent wind came from heaven and filled the whole house where they were sitting.

~ Acts 2:2

WHAT YOU NEED

- page 91, duplicated
- scissors
- tape
- tissue or paper towel tube

BEFORE CLASS

Duplicate a pattern page for each child. Make a sample craft to show the children.

WHAT TO DO

1. Tell the story of Pentecost from Acts chapter 2. Say, **God sent the Holy Spirit down on those who followed Jesus and believed in Him. He sends the Holy Spirit for His people today, too. The Holy Spirit is the Spirit of God. The Spirit helps us live for God, speak to others about Him and serve God.**
2. Show the children the sample craft.
3. Distribute a pattern page to each child.
4. Say the memory verse.
5. Have the children cut the six strips from the page.
6. Show where to tape the strips on one end of the tube.
7. Have the students fold each strip a little. Then have the children hold their noise makers still. Say, **The Holy Spirit came on God's people with a mighty wind and flames of fire on the day of Pentecost. Today, God sends each of us the Spirit in a quiet way when we become His child.**
8. Show how to wave the noise makers and make the sound of a rushing wind.

EXTRA TIME

Have the children read verses 17 and 21. Say, **God promises to give His Spirit to all His people. What promise does God give us in verse 21?**

 ake a noise maker to imitate the
sound of the mighty rushing
wind like God sent at Pentecost.

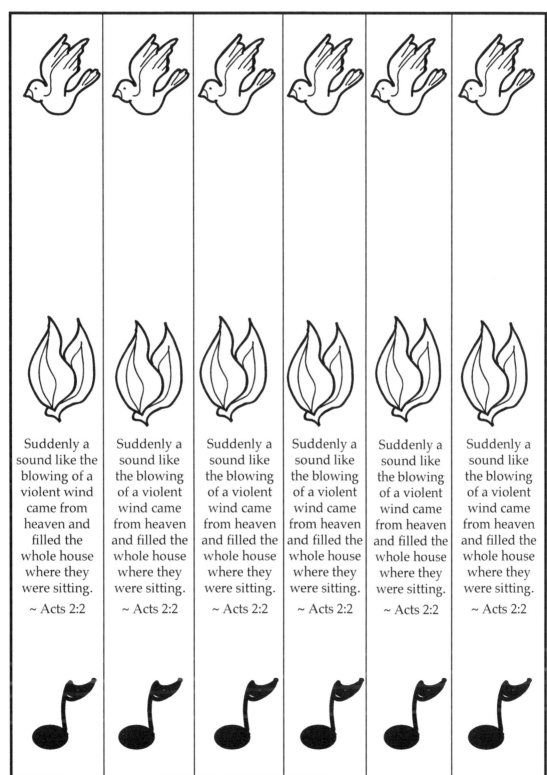

Suddenly a sound like the blowing of a violent wind came from heaven and filled the whole house where they were sitting.

~ Acts 2:2

PAUL AND SILAS IN PRISON
ACTS 16:16-40

MEMORY VERSE

About midnight, Paul and Silas were praying and singing hymns to God.

~ Acts 16:25

WHAT YOU NEED

- page 93, duplicated
- crayons or markers
- pencils

BEFORE CLASS

Duplicate a pattern page for each child.

WHAT TO DO

1. Introduce the lesson by telling the story from Acts 16:16-40. Say, **When troubles come into our lives, we seem to want to whine and complain. Paul and Silas didn't do that. They prayed and sang praises to God. That's because they trusted God to take care of them. If we trust God and pray to Him when we have troubles, our troubles will seem to go away, too!**
2. Distribute a pattern page to each child.
3. Say the memory verse.
4. Have the children write a poem or prayer to praise God.
5. Allow the children to read their poems or prayers aloud if they choose. Let the children color the page as time allows.

EXTRA TIME

Make a praise bulletin board. Have each child write one poem and one prayer on duplicated pages. Put them onto your bulletin board. If time allows, have the children draw a praise picture to be displayed also.

Five Minute

Paul and Silas praised God even in prison. Write a praise poem to God.

Acts 16:16-40

JOHN SEES HEAVEN
BOOK OF REVELATION

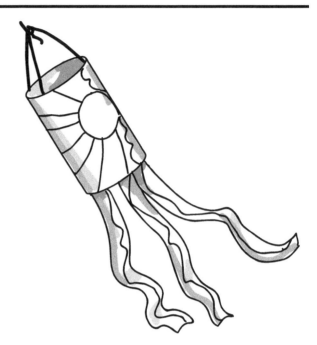

MEMORY VERSE

He made it known by sending his angel to his servant John.

~ Revelation 1:1

WHAT YOU NEED

- page 95, duplicated
- crayons or markers
- construction paper
- scissors
- tape
- yarn
- hole punch

BEFORE CLASS

Duplicate a pattern page for each child. Make a sample craft to show the children.

WHAT TO DO

1. Introduce the lesson by telling the story of John's vision from Revelation. Focus on Revelation 1:1-11. Say, **God allowed John to see a vision of heaven so we will all know the wonderful things to which we can look forward when we get to heaven.**
2. Show the children the sample craft.
3. Distribute a pattern page to each child, and say the memory verse.
4. Have the children cut the windsock from the pattern page.
5. Let the children choose a color of construction paper. They should cut strips from the construction paper that are around 1" x 6".
6. Show how to tape the paper strips along the bottom of the windsock.
7. Show how to roll the windsock into a tube shape, and tape the seam to hold.
8. Instruct the students to tape three lengths of yarn, around 1-foot each, to three places at the top of the windsock. Then tie the three loose ends of the yarn together to form a hanger. Encourage the children to tell what they think heaven will be like and to what they look forward most.

EXTRA TIME

Sing the hymn "Holy, Holy, Holy" with the children. Have the children open their Bibles and find Revelation 4:8b, and read the words that are also contained in the song.

ake a beautiful windsock to remember how wonderful it must have been for John to see heaven in a vision.

He made it
known by
sending
his angel to his
servant John.
~ Revelation 1:1

PUZZLE ANSWERS

page 20

page 26
I drew him out of the water.

page 28

page 34
Your people will be my people and your God my God.

page 40
fear, greed, hate, dishonesty, cheating, selfish, sin, steal, lying, worship idols

page 50

page 56

page 67
gold, incense, myrrh

page 71

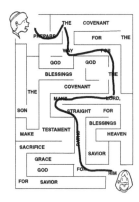

page 79

Down	Across
1. Zacchaeus'	2. tax
3. welcomed	4. sinner
5. four	6. Jesus
6. Jericho	8. sycamore-fig
7. salvation	9. half
	10. lost

page 81

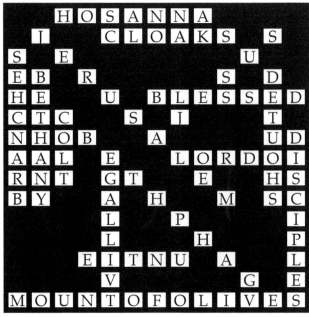

page 87
He has risen! He is not here.